For Jacob.

May you always follow
your dream.

Nandi

In a small town, full of love, Jacob, a very special boy, sits on his bed daydreaming about becoming the President of the United States.

His walls are covered with posters of past presidents, the American flag, and pictures of the White House.

Jacob tells his older brother, Gavin, about his big dreams. Gavin chuckles and says,

"That's great, little bro, but presidents don't just appear out of nowhere. You've got to start small."

Jacob talks to his Mom about wanting to make a difference, just like a president. She smiles warmly and says,

"Why don't you start by helping out here at home?"

He thinks about his mother's words, wondering what helping around the house has to do with being a leader.

She considers her son carefully, then says, "You don't become president by ignoring the little things."

Jacob decides to put his new understanding into action by helping around the house.

He starts with small chores—washing dishes, cleaning his room, and even offering to check the mail without being asked.

Though at first it feels like simple work, Jacob notices how much his mom appreciates it and how it makes home life easier.

He starts to feel proud, seeing how small efforts make a big difference and how thankful his mom is for the help.

GROCERY

Feeling inspired, Jacob wonders how he can contribute to his community.

He walks around his neighborhood and notices a few places that could use help—like the community garden, the park that needs cleaning, and the elderly neighbor who struggles with groceries.

Jacob talks to Gavin about his ideas. Gavin encourages him to gather some friends and start making changes.

Jacob recruits his best friends to help with the park cleanup, and they work together to pick up litter, clean benches, and sweep the walkways.

People in the community notice the boys working hard and thank them for making the park nicer for everyone.

Jacob feels a growing sense of pride, realizing that making an impact in his neighborhood is just as important as big presidential changes.

Not everything goes smoothly—one of Jacob's friends doesn't show up, and they run out of cleaning supplies.

Jacob feels frustrated and wonders if he's really cut out to be a leader.

Gavin reminds Jacob that even presidents face challenges, but what matters is how they respond to setbacks. He reminds Jacob that all of this should be done with love and understanding.

Jacob decides to stay focused and work with what they have, learning how to adapt and keep the project moving forward.

GARDEN

Next, Jacob organizes a group to help plant flowers in the community garden. This time, more people from the town volunteer, inspired by what they saw him do at the park.

The garden project becomes a success, with everyone working together to make the space beautiful.

Jacob feels the satisfaction of leadership—not from giving orders, but from inspiring others to work as a team.

As Jacob reflects on everything he's done—helping around the house, cleaning the park, and working on the garden—he realizes that being president is about more than just speeches and politics.

It's about responsibility, teamwork, and caring for your community.

Jacob smiles to himself and says, "Maybe one day, I'll be president. But for now, I'm making a difference right here."

GROCERY

What Jacob loved most, was
it seemed everyone was
being a little bit
more kind.

Jacob thought, " being President was really just about leading by example!"

And that kindness and love,
always solved problems.
He was seeing that change
every single day and he felt it
in his heart.

It was as if the whole
town were inspired
by one
incredible boy.

As Jacob and his mom settled in for the evening, she knelt beside his bed to reflect on the day.

"I am thankful for this town, thankful for Gavin and our family.

But most of all, I'm thankful for you, Mom."

"We are all learning to love one another better, because oif you."

Jacob's mom kissed his cheek.

"Well, I learned it from you, Mom."
Jacob said sleepily as she turned
off the light.

A heartfelt dedication to the incredible artists whose creativity and passion have graced the canvas, including but not limited to: Niche Watercolor, Value Investor, Art Masalyn, Wulano, Memayu, Nabilah Cholila, Sarina Darin, Asrul Agroni, Visula Co, Julia Bogdan, Sitripatuli, Elena Sadova, Atstock Production, ToBeeLife, Iryana Daniuk, Alvindo, Sudakarn, BombDesign, and Tanisha Jones. Your artistry continues to inspire and elevate the world of creativity —thank you for sharing your unique vision with us all.

Andi Perry Tremor, is known by many names. A soul mother to many, including her “crew” of animals. She spends most of her time writing books about love and staring at unfinished projects. If you liked this story, there is sure to be more, give us a follow at:

andiperrytremor.com

Love Without Limits,

-A

www.ingramcontent.com/pod-product-compliance
Ingram Content Group UK Ltd.
Pitfield, Milton Keynes, MK11 3LW, UK
UKHW060101300726
14090UKWH00003B/332